SIGNS

Savannah to Key West

by Laura Madeline Wiseman

Zea Books, Lincoln, Nebraska

Signs: Savannah to Key West

Design and Layout: Laura Madeline Wiseman

ISBN 978-1-60962-242-8

Zea Books are published by the University of Nebraska-Lincoln Libraries

Electronic (pdf) editions available online at
http://digitalcommons.unl.edu/zeabooks/
Print edition available from http://www.lulu.com/spotlight/unlib

For Grandpa

TABLE OF CONTENTS

INTRODUCTION

Signs: Savannah to Key West documents my 800-mile, 13-day bicycle ride in 2018-2019. It starts fifty miles outside Savannah, Georgia, and follows the Atlantic coastline to Key West, Florida. The trip culminates in Niceville to visit my grandpa, a military veteran and engineer born in 1924.

I've ridden across the country twice. In 2017, I bicycled the Trans America Bicycle Trail from Astoria, Oregon, to Yorktown, Virginia. In 2018, I bicycled a northern route from Anacortes, Washington, to Bar Harbor, Maine. Between those cross-country rides, I followed the Mississippi and other rivers from Muscatine, Iowa, to Baton Rouge, Louisiana. I bicycled the Route 66 Bicycle trail from Chicago to Los Angeles. I have participated in organized rides such as RAGBRAI, GOBA, and Tour de Nebraska.

I plan logistics, journal, log data, and write on such journeys. My bicycle journeys became the books *Great River Legs*, *What a Bicycle Can Carry*, *A Bicycle's Echo*, *Velocipede*, and *Safety Measures*. Often, the books focus on assignments I give myself. On my first cross-country adventure, I sought to find something abandoned on the road each day. These treasures tell the story of the journey. For *Signs*, I photographed signs while I pedaled. The signs focus and structure the story's narrative.

To bike long-distance, assistance helps. I biked the miles in *Signs* with a support driver, my husband, and a long-time bicycle companion. We meet up for breaks, bicycle maintenance, and fuel. Sports technology also helps. For *Signs*, I upgraded to a smartphone, combining a flip phone and iPod setup, and a smartwatch, combining a cyclometer and fitness watch. Together, the upgrades replaced damaged tech and offered much—music, audiobooks, camera, location shares, maps, and data collection. These logged the route and mileage, which appear daily and in the appendix.

To make a book means taking experiences and making a narrative, story, and creative response. Signs function as the bind. Each multi-section poem focuses on one day and the photographed signs collected that day.

Each section focuses on one sign, with two poems that respond to that sign. Sections titles name the sign. Each section is structured as follows:

1) *Prose, Found, Word-Bank Poem* – Using the sign as a found word-bank, each word appears in that order in the prose.
2) *Acrostic Variation* – The first word on each line completes a sign's message.
3) *Character Constraint* – The acrostic and prose poems adhere to a word restriction based on the character count of the sign.

Other structures and constraints bind the poems to invite creative play, magic, and mystery—and this is why I write: the play. I bicycle to know the importance of place.

In 1987, my grandparents moved to Niceville, Florida, to retire. My grandpa enlisted in 1945. He completed his civil and architectural engineering degree from Georgetown in 1946, then served as a commander of a construction battalion that built bridges and airports in Vietnam. My grandparents married in 1951. The photographs of my grandparents' wedding show him in military uniform and her in white tulle. Family photos of their seven children detail the place and time. They often moved—Guam, Pennsylvania, Florida, Illinois, Washington, California, Mississippi, New York, and Hawaii. When my grandpa retired from the military in 1970, they moved to Ohio. He worked as a civil and architectural engineer for the University of Dayton, running the physical plant on campus, and maintaining and constructing buildings. During pre-school through second grade, we lived in the area. I learned to ride a bicycle on their street.

We visited my grandparents in Florida when I was seventeen. They bought our airplane tickets and treated us to fresh squeezed orange juice, commissary shopping, golf cart rides, and beaches. Grandpa sang as he did the crossword. Grandma organized a grandparent family portrait. She talked about cancer and chemotherapy, but only a little. We never saw her again.

In the aftermath, we nearly lost Grandpa, but my aunts and uncles, plus their spouses and children, stayed the loss. First one, then another flew or drove to help, including Grandpa's youngest daughter, my namesake. Even my husband and I visited in 2007. My aunt told stories. My grandpa sang, "La de da da da," over the crossword. My aunt took us to the beach. My grandpa made us sweet-n-sour chicken, saying things like, "Hey honey, can you hand me the doohickey?" We savored the percussive sounds of their voices—my grandpa's commodious tone, my uncle's wheezing laugh, and my aunt's vocal cadence.

Then Grandpa's health had a couple of scares. While on a bike ride, we visited my aunt in Dayton, and she said, "He won't be here much longer." When the company she worked for folded, he sold her house in Ohio, moved to Florida, and helped her sister, my namesake, care for Grandpa, who had been there for him for eleven years. When I wrote about a visit, she said, "He'll be glad to see you."

Rather than planning the usual Midwest holiday circuit seeing family and friends and navigating Nebraska's brutal winters, we planned a bike journey along the Atlantic Coast, then on the way home, a stop in Niceville. We dreamt ocean as we commuted to work, struggling through early December—black ice, city busses sliding, side streets locked in the refrozen melt. When break arrived, we drove and car-camped to Georgia. We pedaled into Savannah, holiday lights bright and streets burbling with festive revelers. We eased our way down the coast for thirteen days, site-seeing and bicycling Florida's bike lanes, bike trails, and multi-use paths. In Key West, we lingered on the beach with Cuban sandwiches and baby oranges, then drove through the night to Niceville to spend a couple of days with my grandpa, aunts, and uncle. A few days after we got back home, my grandpa died. He was nearly 95. He had lived a long life full of words, family, and travel. As I write this, today would have been his 98th birthday.

A bicycle carries a rider through place. The voices of family carry us back and forth through time. I am grateful for the journey that ended with a welcome visit. As a little girl riding big wheels up and down my grandpa's street, drinking the juice Grandma always had in the fridge, and sitting in the den with them—her reading and him doing the crossword—are memories that hold me.

Laura Madeline Wiseman, Ph.D.
Lincoln, Nebraska
January 27th, 2022

DAY 1: BREAK STARTS ON BICYCLE

Denmark to Savannah, Georgia

Saturday, December 15, 2018 – 50 miles

1. Welcome to Georgia

o

The road **welcomes** us into winter break. We turn-take driving, doing the crossword, playing audiobooks, or singing lyrics, "La de, dah da da dah."

"Should we reread that Hemingway book, *Old Man and the Sea?*"

"Sure."

The rental murmurs with supplies—mandarins, tires, tubes, sunscreen, beer. Highway traffic pulses. We car camp mid-route to finish the drive from Nebraska **to** Georgia. Our 800-mile bicycle route goal awaits: a long curl along the Atlantic seacoast for winter break—Savannah to Key West.

"What will we do in Savannah?"

"Whatever we want."

"We, or one of our siblings, almost went to school here, right?"

"Yeah." We study our phones. One of our siblings is getting a divorce.

White bolls stand on dried stocks in the fields of **Georgia**. Dampness hazes the air with softness. Birds call. "My grandpa was born in Atlanta. He went to Georgetown."

"Yeah?" Traffic careens.

"Let's get Lexa ready." We bike check and pre-ride stretch, then check the map.

"How should we organize the trip until we see my grandpa, aunts, and uncle—by the signs?"

"Sure."

"Should we count them?"

Nodding towards the first with a kiss: "**Welcome to Georgia**."

o

"Welcome into Chippewa Square. Let's

toast." Lifting hands, "To Grandpa." "To his **Georgia**." Then we ask, "Motel-it?"

DAY 2: FIRST SIGNS OF GEORGIA

Statesboro to Odum, GA

Sunday, December 16, 2018 – 71 miles

1. Thank you for driving slowly

o

"The [town]-[town] road signs are cool. **Thank you**."

"**For** real? For what?"

"**Driving** us crazy."

"Sure."

Hot, **slowly,** and steadily, we kiss today's start: Jones-Countryclub Road.

o

"**Thanks**," We tell the clerk.
You unfold gum wrappers for us. "Nice gal,
for letting us both use the men's."
Driving us crazy, we kiss again,
slowly. "What's next?"

2. Caution bridge may ice in winter

o

Yesterday's miles **caution** us. We adjust Lexa's triangle to cross **bridge**s. It's December, not **May.** In Nebraska, dangerous **ice** staggers vehicles. **In** Georgia, our **winter** break whispers with birds.

"Good?"

"Yes—ladadada."

o

Cautioned by traffic and seamed
bridges, orchards inspire our:
"Maybe, let's get pecans,

iced tea, and peaches?" We search
internet reviews. "Sure.
Winter break means we can do whatever we want."

3. Emergency Dial 911

o

A red admiral butterfly lands. With **emergency**, her mouth **dial**s the bicycle glove. "Is this her **911** hunger?"

o

"**Emergency**. Traffic sucks," we text.
Dialing a "Sup—need anything?"
"**911** or more defensive training for loggers."

4. Woodpecker Trail 121

o

Woodpeckers flash in the trees. You **trail** after me, "Good?"
I fight rumble strips. "What if he lived to **121**?"

o

Woodpeckers sing. You
trail after me. Then in room
121, we motel-it with PBS documentaries, mandarins, and beer.

DAY 3: SOME MORE ANNOUNCEMENTS

Odum to Folkston, GA, plus Chesser Island Boardwalk
Monday, December 17, 2018 – 71 miles

1. Thank You Blue

o

"**Thank**s." **You** flushed the cockroach down our motel room's toilet. **Blue** water whirled.

o

"**Thank**s." Last night,
you helped us with Lexa,
blue light singing above.

2. Odum Shooting Preserve Tower Pheasant Hunts Quail Hunts

o

Odum's trucks terrorized bicyclers. Last night, trucks drilled. Workers **shot** glances at the church **tower** near which we'd parked. We secured Lexa and **preserve**d her freewheel. "See any **pheasant** or **hunt**ers?"

"On these roads—pheasants, **quail**, bicycle—equally **hunt**ed."

Then we motel-ed it with movies. "Remember Hemingway's Chicago home?"

"That Oak Park tour we did?"

"Sure."

o

Odum gets us breakfast among locals,
shooting the breeze. Today, a
preserve on our itinerary—sea turtles—and a
tower, too, this one for alligators. We ride.
Pheasants lift from gumtrees. Autos
hunt the roads, growling in the morning.

Quail peck the ditches trembling with gumtree stars. Still
hunting, automobiles snarl at traffic lights.

3. Water Over Road

o

Water fingers runnels of backroads, mirroring **over**cast hues. "Ditch the main **road**?"

"Sure."

o

Water fingers drive. Water froths ditches.
Overflow swirls. Which [town]-[town]
roads lead us to sea turtles?

4. 20 LB ICE

o

"A **20 lb** bag of **ICE** for the beer."

o

"**20**
lb bag of mandarins, too, please."
"**Ice**—yeah?"

5. Public Safety and Veterans Highway

o

Even with backroads, all-day riding meld **public** and private. What's **safety**? Lexa's triangle dangles, swishing its orange **and** yellow. Loggers shake the roads. If we're long-distance cycling **veterans**, **highway**s still blunt thought.

o

Public displays of kisses unfold us—what's
safety? Will we see alligators? Patrols idle,
and traffic rumbles. So what? Our
veterans

served and built these bridges and roads.
Highways tremble with loggers' trucks, overborne.

6. Keep Georgia Peachy Clean Please Don't Litter

o

We dial, text, and video to **keep** shoulders from locking and the wheel from wavering throughout **Georgia**. "Hi. We're doing **peachy**."

Whine: food, electrolytes, **clean** clothes, fewer layers. "Please."

"Need something—a break?"

"Sure. **Don't** think about it."

"Yeah?"

"Why all the roadside **litter**."

o

Keeping to it, we practice mindfulness:
Georgian elementary kids burbling
peachy orchards glimmering
clean roadways careening.
Please. By day 3 of all-day biking, bikers lose it.
"**Don't** think about it," we say. "Why's
litter a sliding fee scale of $1,000 - $1,200?"

7. Welcome if you Own It

o

We're welcomed into cotton-lined backroads**. You** photograph the sunset. We call this our **own**. "**It** could be worse."

"Yeah?"

o

Welcomed into Georgia.
It's our last day cycling here
. Yielding,
we ask, "Rebel flags?" Calling out

our discomfort. "Motel-
it, now?"

DAY 4: FLORIDA'S INITIAL INDICATORS

Folkston, GA, to American Beach, Florida

Tuesday, December 18, 2018 – 63 miles

1. Florida

o

Cockroaches mushed, and we dream into **Florida.**

o

Awakened, we ride. **Florida**'s sign appears fenced.

2. Florida enforces speed limits

o

We text, "**Florida**!" Traffic **enforces** our shoulder-hugging. It **speed**s along. We pause to adjust layers. An osprey pleats her nest of blanched sticks on a platform.

"Off **limits**?"

"Yeah."

o

Florida's Hemingway via audiobook
enforces literary reconsideration. We tried his movie
at mandarin and beer
speed last night but stopped. Our
limits? Him beating a fish with his fists.

3. FDOT Test Message

o

FDOT's litmus? Skills **test:** broken shoulders crowd with barriers. We **message**, "Good?"

"Traffic." Grandpa built better roads.

o

FDOT's other litmus? Skills
test: blogger maps to spot wildlife. We
message photos, "Look, manatees like silhouettes."

4. Slow down my mommy works here

o

"Swamp next?"

Slow and steady, we kiss. **Down**ed by so much riding, we say, "Sure. Oh, **mommy**—la, ha, ha, ha." What **works** out knots? **"Here** we go, a tennis ball."

o

Slow and steady, we press
down into what releases pressure.
My response? "Oh,
mommy." We always press into what
works, then read aloud alligator-spotting tips.
"Here we go. Swamp!"

5. Slow down my daddy works here

o

"Now? It's free after 3 PM."

Slow and steady, we break to touch. "Sure." **Down**ed, **my** legs radiate heat. "Oh, **daddy**," pressing harder. It **works**.

"**Here** we go—alligators!"

o

Slow and steady, we cruise
down the park loop.
My body unknots. "Oh,
daddy." It is what
works. "Numbered posts?
Here we go—alligator tour, then motel, okay?"

DAY 5: MORE NOTICES

American Beach to Palm Coast, FL

Wednesday, December 19, 2018 – 78 miles

1. Peds and Bikes Only

o

Our day ahead: **peds** trail, breweries, **and** seagulls. "Just like riding **bikes.**"

"Sure."

Only thing: breaking sleep to kiss.

o

"**Peds** trail?" we message.
Just like riding our
bikes, it's, "Beachwalk?"
Only thing—our holding hands.

2. Right Lane Only

o

Right. Text: "Sunrise?" On **lane**d sand—trucks, chairs, beachcombers. **Only** thing: mandarin-hued surf and sky.

o

Right. Lexa
lanes through miles. Then it's dusk.
Only things left—motel, brewery, and news.

3. Unlawful to pick Sea Oats

o

Unlawful? Maybe. **To** snore through it? To **pick** "0" for the front desk? To break their family's **sea** vacation? "Oh, **oats**." The kid upstairs starts again.

o

Unlawful—what happens next.

To tire her out, the mom
picks the parking lot. The kid runs in circles.
Seagulls rise, flapping. Oh,
oats—her keening.

DAY 6: ZERO DAY

Kennedy Space Center, FL

Thursday, December 20, 2018 – zero day

1. NASA

o

We text, "Try **NASA**?"

o

Then after, "**NASA** accomplished."

DAY 7: TODAY'S SIGNS FOR YESTERDAY

Oak Hill to Palm Coast, FL

Friday, December 21, 2018 – 58 miles

1. Warning Crime Watch Area New Smyrna Beach Call 911

o

Yesterday, storm **warnings** triggered our, "NASA?"

"In the rain?"

"Sure."

NASA's **crime**: fees. At Kennedy Space Center, we **watch**ed the near-empty parking **area**. "Why's it $10 to park?"

"It's **new**?"

"Let's not break-up with Lexa."

Smyrna Beach storms on our phones. "**Call** it?"

"**911**, NASA. No bicycles, so rockets?"

o

Warnings triggered. Our
crime? Tiptoeing through mulched beds,
watching personal bubbles, avoiding overcrowded
areas. The Rock Garden Tour included
new rockets. The tour guide babbled.
Smyrna Beach stormed—all
beaches stormed, even NASA's. Some
call us crazy for loving bicycles. We called
911, all pretend, "Hi, NASA, we're crazy. Rockets."

2. No fishing from bridge

o

No kidding. "Burgers at Obit Café?" **Fishing** for something terrestrial from NASA, we ask, "Alligator burgers?"

"Maybe—where? There's a **bridge** burger?"

o

No kidding. We burgered it,
fishing for our next thing on our phones.
From there, we toured
the bridges of rockets.

3. No parking any time

o

No kidding. **Parking** ourselves in line, we joined the throng. "**Any** chance we'll see it?"

"It's scheduled."

"What **time**?"

o

No kidding. 30-40 minutes. Still
parking it, queued up for Mars.
Any movement thrilled. "What
time's the next thing?"

4. Stay off dune beach dune restoration progress use crosswalks and designated beach access areas

o

Stay with us, reader. Mars exhibit finished**, and** we booked it to the IMAX. "First 'Journey to Mars,' then a bus tour through NASA's **dune beach**es." Then it started to get weird.

"**Dune**s?"

"**Restoration** project—I think."

"Sure."

Storms **progress**ed**.** We skirted puddles and **use**d the **crosswalks**. Rainclouds grumbled **and** patterned the covered **sidewalks**. Door greeters welcomed NASA-goers like us into **designated** theaters.

"Let's **beach** it at the top."

We scored seats with aisle **access** and dabbed raindrops from our faces. The theater filled. Near the doors, parking **areas** for strollers and kid carts filled.

o

Stay with us, reader. Before the film even started
off, people started munching—praline pecans, lorna
dunes, cheddar sunbaked wheat squares.
Beach bags, diaper bags, and themed sandpiper
dune bags opened. NASA-goers started personal
restoration projects to snack. Our tongues
progressed against the wet seeds of pomegranates.
Useful NASA workers stood everywhere—
crosswalks, entrances, interior theater doors—
and held the door for all. Never having such
designated permission, we welcomed the theater's dimming.
Beach vistas started NASA's film of Martian
access. "Grandma liked praline pecans." We scan seated
areas, "and pouring peanuts into the lid."

5. Beach warning flags water closed public high hazards high surf and/or strong currents medium hazard moderate surf and/or currents low hazard calm conditions exercise caution dangerous marine line

o

Storms triggered more **warning**s. Our white **flags** lifted. Rain**water** streamed. After IMAX, we boarded the tour bus. It hissed as the doors **closed**, and the **public** snacking began. **High** in our front row seats, we saw as the driver saw. "**Hazard,** she's seen it all?"

High and half-hidden, we fished half-eaten pomegranates from our bag. Our tongues **surf**ed the honeycomb runnels **and/or** broke the seeds.

Strong waves lashed the dunes. Wind **currents** pushed dune grass around. We jolted over NASA's wet vistas. Like a **medium**, she predicted our questions, "I'll tell you about ______."

"**Hazard**, she'd said it all before?"

Surf curled. Puddles puzzled the roads. Stopping **and/or** jerking to check for alligators, the bus expelled exhaust **currents**. We hunkered **low**.

"**Hazard,** she'd seen them **calm**?"

Storm **conditions** dissuaded alligators, she said. They liked to **exercise** in the warmth, she said. This is why she drove with **caution**, she said. Then she started repeating herself. "I already said that," she said. **Dangerous**-sized trucks stood unmoved by the winds. "Now, since I told you that already, I'll tell you _____."

We tongued pomegranates. The **marine** reflected a yellow back sky. When did public snacking become the **line**?

o

Beach loop of NASA completed, and alligator trigger-
warnings missed, we arrived. Our white
flags lifted. Sidewalks of puddles,
watery and leaf-littered, but not
closed, the rocket museum remained open—
restrooms, gift shops, and films.
High up on the public's agenda? Want to
hazard a guess? Public eating remained
high. We circuited the rooms,
surfing exhibits of astronaut gear
and/or interactive play where touch was a
strong lesson. "Touch the moon rock."
Storm currents shifted. Light rain became
medium, got crazy, then crazier still.
Hazard a guess? People snacked.
Moderate wind sang. "Next up—NASA, motel, and beer?" We
surfed our phones. "Maybe—there's a motel with a space theme,

and/or we could try to catch the last astronaut talk, then go?"
Currents of wind exhaled, long and slow.
Low on ideas, we queued for the bus.
Hazard a guess: yep, snacking in line
calms all. "Souvenirs?" Then storm
conditions tumbled everything from the displays.
Exercise? We sprinted to the bus. The driver's
cautions of alligators vanished. The bus sprinted us
dangerously to "Legends and Heroes," that
marine drop from space. What does an astronaut's
life miss most? The spaceman sang, "Bye, bye, apple pie."

DAY 8: SIGNPOSTS AS PSA

Oak Hill to Melbourne Shores, FL

Saturday, December 22, 2018 – 68 miles

1. Florida Highway Patrol Dial

o

Florida starts us bundled for the **highway**. Palm trees line the road, and **patrol**s abound. We **dial** and text. "Route looks safe."

"SpaceX rocket launch ahead!"

o

Florida starts us riding near NASA's
highways. Near NASA's beaches**,**
patrols in blue uniforms fill SUVs.
Dialing, we ask, "Seems safe, yeah? A real rocket ship today?"

2. No Motor Vehicles

o

No kidding. **Motor**s give bicycles three-feet of space. **Vehicles** pass in the other lane. We text, "Scrubbing?"

o

No kidding. Bicycle trails appear.
Motors line the roadways and lots.
Vehicles park everywhere. "Or counting down?"

3. Florida Greenways and Trails System Trail Town Florida Department of Environmental Protection

o

We ride **Florida**'s rocket traffic. **Greenways** teem. Parking lots **and** roadsides swarm. We **trail** after each other, following the state's **system**. We

trail after rockets, listening for the next broadcast. "Who's the **town** bicycle—rockets, traffic, or us?"

"Yeah—bump, bump, bah da."

Some **Florida** beaches stay wild behind fences, open water glimmering a deep, dark blue. Some **department** protects pelicans, manatees, and sea oats.

Of course, we ride, even if **environmental** storms could scrub the mission. Our mission is Lexa **protection** and mid-ride breaks for local beer and mandarins.

o

Florida transforms as we ride. Suburban solitude becomes
greenways jammed with GPS 3 watchers.
Near liftoff amid the hoards, we text, "Launching?"
Trailing after each other, we gush over NASA's live stream
system check—hydrogen, oxygen, mechanics.
Trailing after rockets, we text, "Sure." Maybe we're both
town bicycles. Then, our burbling stops, "Sadness,
Florida." Storms scrubbed NASA's SpaceX
departmental launch. Not a divorce or cancer,
of course, just logistics. We listen—storms overseas,
environmental hazards, personnel
protection. We hug and kiss. "Next rocket, okay?"

4. Evacuation Route

o

As if **evacuation** orders sounded, rocket crowds vanish. Greenways empty. Highways silence. Our **route** calms.

o

"**Evacuation**—did Grandpa ever?" We text tonight's
route. "We once waited out tornadoes in his basement."

5. Slow Flooded Area No Wake

o

Slow and steady. We still get **flooded** by trafficked **area**s. **No** kidding.

"Let's beach it and nap."

"Okay."

"**Wake** us in ten, okay?"

o

Slow and steady, we cruise once
flooded sections,
built areas, then rebuilt again.
No kidding. We text, "Mini-naps
wake us up—one more beach?"

6. Bike Lane

o

Just like riding **bikes**, we follow **lane**s to ocean.

o

Bikes—just like riding one—
lane to our motel.

DAY 9: RED AND YELLOW FLAGS

Melbourne Shores to Jensen Beach, FL
Sunday, December 23, 2018 – 67 miles

1. Don't Drive Intexticated

o

Don't think about it. Sometimes things break. NASA reschedules. Rockets **drive** us crazy. We get to it, biking **intexticated.** "What time's the rescheduled launch?"

o

Don't think about it, Lexa. Today's pre-launch Florida traffic
drives us crazy. Everywhere, vehicles move, half-
intexticated, searching for rockets inside their phones.

2. Learn to Surf Rent a Board Bike Sup

o

While we **learn** places **to** view rockets, we **surf** miles by bicycle. Beach **rent**al shops sing with **board**s, cruisers, sun umbrella/chair combos. Just like riding a **bike**, we text, "**Sup**? Beach it in twenty?"

o

Learning Florida—our break
to not think about it—we
surf spots for breaks:
rental stops or bicycling stops,
any stop an astronaut might
board. Just like riding a
bike, we text,
"**Sup**? Countdown yet?"

3. State Park Marina

o

State it: biking is a walk in the **park**, and rocket-watching is a chase toward a **marina**.

o

State it. Let's get our walk in the
park for rockets, if
marinas storm, we'll try again.

4. No Dogs Allowed in Park

o

No kidding. Rockets **dog-**tire us. "Scrubbed or **allowed**?"
Then, we text like kids, "**In** the air."
"A walk in the **park**."
"Yeah."

o

No kidding. Our
dog-tired selfies are
allowed. It's our walk
in the—rocket, ocean, beach—
park. Our rocket-launch-mandarin-beer treat.

5. Break the Grip of the Rip

o

Rocket launched. Now we ride into Palm Beach. Never **break**ing **the** paceline, other cyclists **grip** handlebars and push. **Of** course, **the** safety triangle **rip**s loose.

o

Breaking in Palm Beach—
there's nowhere to potty.
Gripping Lexa, hunkering,

we're invisible, of course
(**the** outclassed). Fancy vehicles
rip around us, driving (in class).

6. No Parking No Standing Any Time

o

No kidding, we text later, "Sometimes nobody's **parking** on some beaches."

"Did you see the president's hotel?" **No** kidding.

"Somebody was **standing** there, taking photos, **any**way."

"What **time**?"

"Noon?"

"Sure."

o

No kidding. Sometimes there's evidence of breakage.
Parking-it in the motel later—with our phones—
no kidding—we play distraction games.
Standing activity? Search.
"**Any** more rockets? What
time?"

7. Do Not Take Land Crabs

o

"**Do** you give that kid a second thought?"

"As often as **not**."

We **take** selfies. "Do rockets **land** among the **crabs**?

"Sure."

o

"**Do** you feel bad for that whole family?"
"As often as **not**."
"**Take** a good selfie.

Landscape?" Do only
crabs dial "0"?

8. No Fishing Within Park Boundaries

o

No kidding. **Fishing** for more distraction breaks, we ask, "Remember that swamp tower?" **within** milliseconds, adding, "Our walk/bike in the park to spot alligators along the **boundaries** of water and light?"

"Sure."

o

No kidding. To alligator-spot in Georgia meant
fishing around wildlife areas. "But maybe,"
within milliseconds, it's, "a walk in the everglades
park?" We study our phones—the mapped
boundaries. "Isn't NPS shut down?"

9. Drop off No Dogs be Safe and Nice Tides High Low

o

Back to riding: **dropping** trash into a bin right **off** a beach—**no** kidding—we text, "Love Florida's public trash."

We text, "**Dog**-tired. You?"

"**Be**tter—what's **safe** ahead for a break?"

"**And nice.**"

A naval audiobook murmurs. We ride towards **tides** flagged red. "**High** alert?"

"Yeah. **Low**'s yellow."

o

Drop riding. Let's back
off. We motel-it.
No kidding. Sketchy. One guy
dog-tires us. Another gal in

beads sashays by—what's
safe? Lexa watches the door.
"**And** Palm Beach—it's
nice." Something like flagged
tide breaks against our door. "They're
high?" Staying
low, we wake our phones.

10. Indiana River No Swimming or Diving No Fishing from Bridge

o

Ride: "Why **Indiana**?" We question everything. "**River** or barrier island?" We find half-boarded-up motels. **No** kidding. No **swimming** here. No beaches **or** drinking. No **diving**. We find housing remnants—cement foundation, rebar, and iron gate. "Flooded?"

"Hurricaned."

No kidding. "Are relators **fishing** for anyone willing?" **From** there, we follow it up a **bridge**. We understand nothing.

o

Indiana or Florida?
River or ocean?
No kidding. Back to the motel. Not a soul
swimming, not even a kid
or a hot-tubber,
diving into the deep end.
No kidding. What's worse? Strangers
fishing for something? What would Grandpa think? Or
from that other motel that kid keening? What
bridges another's divorce? What bridges loss? We kiss.

DAY 10: INDICATORS OR WARNINGS

Jensen Beach to Briny Breezes, FL

Monday, December 24, 2018 – 65 miles

1. Ahead

o

Ahead, mangroves sing with pigeons.

o

Ahead, the president's daylit hotel.

2. Road Flooded

o

The **road** says **flooded** but sounds sketchy. That's what we text, "Sketchy."

o

Road cruised by police. "Need a break?"
"**Flooded**?" We text, "A little."

3. Please Stay off Ramp Lifeguard Use Only

o

Please. **Stay** with us, reader. One guy rolls into a restroom. No toilet on or **off**, no splash of tap, no toilet paper rolls. On the **ramp,** another guy reclines. No **lifeguard**s here. **Only** thing: we hold our potty.

o

Please. Shut the curtains.
(**Stay** with us, reader.) Last night—
frenetic sprinklers and jiggling doorknobs.
Ramped up, that gal sashayed the halls. Lexa
lifeguarded. Unknown touches
used our door, broke against it.
Only thing to do? Phone searches.

DAY 11: WHAT ISN'T SIGNED

Briny Breezes to Kendall, FL

Tuesday, December 25, 2018 – 73 miles

1. Briny Breezes Gulf Streams Park M-Path East Coast Greenway

o

Our day breaks. Miami's **briny breezes** call you, while my **gulf streams** feature exploded trash bags. You **park** on the beach far from my **M-Path.** On yours, storms **east** push stingrays into the shallows. Lifeguards flag purple. On mine, men **coast greenway**s on bicycles with low seats strapped with milkcrates, kickstand them on the trail, or wobble nearby.

o

Briny surf burbles with kids, but
breezes can't stir cardboard housing.
Gulf chatters with parents, but
traffic streams can't stop men who
park in hoodies, eyes big and red-black. We text,
"**M-path**," pedaling. You beach it
east of where men step, too buoyant.
Coasts of umbrellas for you. For me:
greenways of—men slouching, shopping carts, trash.

DAY 12: PROHIBITIONS

Kendall to Islamorada, FL

Wednesday, December 26, 2018 – 60 miles

1. Caution for Your Safety

o

"Use **caution**," we text. Explored trash bags appear for miles. **For** real. **Your** tactic matches my own: grip the wheel. What's **safety**?

o

Caution. We ride amid graffiti.
For real. "I'm close,"
your text. Commuter lots, shadowy buildings—what's
safety? Trash dumped (or salvaged?).

2. No Lifeguard on Duty Swim at Your Own Risk

o

No kidding—Lexa serves as **lifeguard**, or maybe **on duty** Samaritan, and **swims**, sinks, or drowns **at** a bus kiosk where men with shopping carts hover. **Your** idle. "Should Lexa ride this?"

Calling it our **own**, we text, "We're **risk**ing it."

o

No kidding. Another vehicle runs interference,
lifeguards when a shopping cart veers
onto Lexa's path. Where's the police on
duty? At Last Chance,
swimming with SUVs,
"**Your** call. This is our
own ride." It's a
risk, yes. It's better than some things.

3. Pets are Not Allowed on Beach

o

At Last Chance, beach-bound **pets** wait. "**Are** you pottying?"
"As often as **not**. Is a snack **allowed**?"
On Highway 1, traffic growls. "We're going to the **beach**."
"Yeah."

o

"**Pets**—do bicycles count?"
"**Are** you biking?"
"As often as **not**." What recovery is
allowed? We check Lexa's tires.
On tap? Somewhere—key lime
beaches, mandarins, and beer.

4. Consumption of Alcoholic Beverages Prohibited

o

Consumption of snacks complete, we ride Highway 1. **Of** course, signs flash alligator warnings. Traffic roars. The cacophony ricochets—fences, bridges, rumble strips. Of course, **alcoholic**-themed shops blaze—**beverages** available, exit now. We blink. Thoughts **prohibited.** We listen. Audiobooks jabber. We breathe. Sea mirrors storm.

o

Consumption of ales at a brewery entertains, eventually.
"**Of** course—key lime on a stick," we text, then list other
alcoholic key lime options. Stretching, we message,
"**Beverages,** too, like at the Nebraska State Fair?"
Prohibited from stopping long at each break, we kiss. "Storms?"

5. Recycle Aluminum Plastic Glass

o

The aquarium's **recycl**ing kiosk welcomes. "Any **aluminum** cans?" We tidy the rental, "Or **plastic**?" Side-stepping broken **glass**, we recycle.

"Closed?" We crumple the handout. "No glass-bottomed boat tour?"

"Canceled. Storms."

o

Recycle work complete, we leisure near tethered
aluminum-bottomed boats. Storm waters sing.
Plastic buoys ride swells. Seagulls stand.
"**Glass** of beer, call Granpa, or motel-it with movies?"

6. Trash

o

"Sure." The Keys welcome **trash**.

o

"**Trash**?" We tidy, then motel.

DAY 13: BIKE SIGNS TO THE END

Islamorada to Key West, FL

Thursday, December 27, 2018 – 84 miles

1. Cut

o

Why paint, "**Cut**"?

o

Cut sleep. Ride.

2. Florida Keys' Overseas Heritage Trail

o

"Last day, **Florida**," we say, following orange-painted **keys** marking cycling paths **overseas.** Legs of it unlock Key West's **heritage** along rails lines. We **trail** after each other. "How can this be winter?"

"It's our winter break."

o

Florida's gift? Wide-shouldered roads.
Keys'? Multi-use trail, shaggy mangroves,
overseas bridges, and islands. We follow this
heritage told in last night's PBS documentary. We text,
trailing after each other, "After this, Grandpa's next, right?"

3. For Your Environment and Protection Park Rules

o

For real. Our rendezvous starts plotted—potty, coffee, seven-mile bridge. We planned for **your** mandarin smoothie, **environment**s that welcome bikers **and** support drivers, and sun **protection.** Our hello kisses are a walk in the **park**. A chicken **rules** the grass.
"Look, chickens!"
"Look—iguanas?"

o

For real. Post-coffee, traffic thunders.
Your phone seeks oceanic
environments of shallow pools, boats asea,
and bicycles. Winter break travel's our favorite
protection game, and walk in the world's
park. So, if sinus pain and head-splitting pressure
rules, we text, "Break or good?" We're almost there.

4. No Littering

o

No kidding. Not Georgia's **littering** fines: $1,200. Not Florida's: $50. Still.

o

No kidding? Please punish (fine?) that sulfuric stink
littering Key West's air.

5. No Alcohol Consumption

o

No kidding. We skip key lime beer or **alcohol** at lunch, ordering Cuban sandwiches for **consumption.** "Following the rules," we text.

o

No kidding. Like spring break, but no sex,
alcohol, or drugs. No dance party. No
consumption. Nothing naughty here. "It's break, right?"

6. No Tents or Camping

o

No kidding. No **tents** appear. No **camping** in Key West, Miami, the everglades, **or** near the president's hotel. "Beach nap?"

o

No kidding. Elsewhere we've biked,

tents abound—national parks
or state park forests—and car
camping abounded, too.

7. No Tying Off On Structures

o

No kidding. We made it to Key West. We beach it, **tying** awareness to breathing or dozing **off**. **On** the horizon, **structures**—condos, hotels, resort spas?

o

No kidding. We nap.
Tying Lexa to a palm tree
offers sand and sun that go
on and on. Breaking surf
structures our hours.

8. Fires Prohibited

o

"New Year's beach **fires** with Grandpa now?"
We search maps. "Motel-it or car camp?"
"**Prohibited**?"

o

"**Fires** with Grandpa. Sure." We nap, beaching it.
Prohibited? Ending the journey before we're ready.

9. All Pets Must Be Leashed

o

"**All** right?" we text, side-by-side. **Pets** lag beside walkers.
"**Must be**—we've biked it."
Gulls brace. Iguanas tiptoe. Toddlers wade, un**leashed.**
"Goodbye kisses?"

"Sure."

o

All night we drive. Highway growls.
Pets, beaches, Grandpa's,
"**Must** stay—we've got a spare
bedroom." Lexa
leashed. We say, "Let's toast: to the end!"

APPENDIX

Day	Route	Signs	Miles
Day 1	Denmark to Savannah, Georgia	1	50
Day 2	Statesboro to Odum, GA	4	71
Day 3	Odum to Folkston, GA	7	71
Day 4	Folkston, GA to American Beach, Florida	5	63
Day 5	American Beach to Palm Coast, FL	3	78
Day 6	Kennedy Space Center, FL	1	0
Day 7	Oak Hill to Palm Coast, FL	6	58
Day 8	Oak Hill to Melbourne Shores, FL	6	68
Day 9	Melbourne Shores to Jensen Beach, FL	10	67
Day 10	Jensen Beach to Briny Breezes, FL	3	65
Day 11	Briny Breezes to Kendall, FL	1	73
Day 12	Kendall to Islamorada, FL	6	60
Day 13	Islamorada to Key West, FL	9	84
	Totals	**62**	**808**

ACKNOWLEDGMENTS

Thanks to my colleagues and students at the University of Nebraska-Lincoln. Thanks to my husband, Adam Wagler, for his support, love, and generosity.

Thanks to the local, state, country, and world mapmakers, such as Adventure Cycling Association, Google Maps, and the Rails-to-Trails Conservatory. Thanks to those who maintain, support, and protect routes, such as U.S. Bicycle Route 1, Georgia Coast Rail Trail, the Amelia Island Bike Trails, Talbot Island State Park Trails, and Florida Keys Overseas Heritage Trail.

Thanks to the cyclists who ride the bike trails, streets, highways, interstates, and back roads daily. Cycling among these kind, smart, and strong riders has given me the strength to commute year-round, train on an indoor trainer, and adventure supported and self-supported farther than I thought bicycles could go. Learning about the bicycling adventures of this community is the inspiration.

ABOUT THE AUTHOR

Laura Madeline Wiseman is the author of several poetry collections, including *Velocipede,* a Foreword INDIES Book of the Year Award Finalist published by Stephen F. Austin State University Press. Other books of poetry include *What a Bicycle Can Carry, Through a Certain Forest, An Apparently Impossible Adventure, Wake, Some Fatal Effects of Curiosity and Disobedience, Sprung, American Galactic,* and *Queen of the Platform.* Her newest poetry book is *Journey to Nowhere* from Finishing Line Press. Her newest chapbook of poetry is *Diversions* from Dancing Girl Press.

Madeline has collaborated on books with writers, artists, designers, and illustrators, including *Intimates and Fools* and *Leaves of Absence,* both with Sally Deskins. Other collaborative books include *People Like Cats* and *The Hunger of the Cheeky Sisters.* Her newest collaborative chapbook is *Every Girl Becomes the Wolf* with Andrea Blythe, published by Finishing Line Press. She edited two poetry anthologies, *Bared: Contemporary Poetry and Art on Bras and Breasts* and *Women Write Resistance: Poets Resist Gender Violence.* She is the editor of *The Chapbook Interview.*

Madeline is also the author of prose. Her collection of creative nonfiction is *A Bicycle's Echo* published by Red Dashboard. Her newest lyric prose collections are *Great River Legs* and *Safety Measures,* published by Zea Books. Her poetry, fiction, nonfiction, and reviews have appeared in *Margie, Mid-American Review, Poet Lore, Blackbird, Arts & Letters, Prairie Schooner, Feminist Studies, The Iowa Review, Ploughshares,* and *Calyx.*

Madeline earned a B.S. in Women's Studies and English Literature from Iowa State University, an M.A. in Women's Studies from the University of Arizona, and a Ph.D. in English from the University of Nebraska-Lincoln. She recently earned a second M.A. in Integrated Media Communications from the University of Nebraska-Lincoln.

She has received an Academy of American Poets Award, a Louise Van Sickle Fellowship, the Helene Wurlitzer Foundation Fellowship, a Hitchcock Fellowship, and grants from the Kimmel Harding Nelson Center for the Arts and the Center for the Great Plains Studies.

ALSO BY THE AUTHOR

Books

Great River Legs (Zea Books, 2021)
Safety Measures (Zea Books, 2021)
Journey to Nowhere (Finishing Line Press, 2019)
What a Bicycle Can Carry (BlazeVOX [books], 2018)
A Bicycle's Echo (Red Dashboard, 2018)
Through a Certain Forest (BlazeVOX [books], 2017)
Velocipede (Stephen F. Austin State University Press, 2016)
An Apparently Impossible Adventure (BlazeVOX [books], 2016)
Drink (BlazeVOX [books], 2015)
Wake (Aldrich Press, 2015)
American Galactic (Martian Lit Books, 2014)
Some Fatal Effects of Curiosity and Disobedience (Lavender Ink, 2014)
Queen of the Platform (Anaphora Literary Press, 2013)
Sprung (San Francisco Bay Press, 2012)

Collaborative Collections

Yoga Birds with designer Adam Wagler (Zea Books, 2019)
Every Girl Becomes the Wolf with poet Andrea Blythe (Finishing Line Press, 2018)
People like Cats with artist Chuka Susan Chesney (Red Dashboard, 2016)
Leaves of Absence: An Illustrated Guide to Common Garden Affection with artist Sally Deskins (Red Dashboard, 2016)
The Hunger of the Cheeky Sisters: Ten Tales with artist Lauren Rinaldi (Les Femmes Folles Books, 2015)
Intimates and Fools with artist Sally Deskins (Les Femmes Folles Books, 2014)

Edited Collections

Bared: Contemporary Poetry and Art on Bras and Breasts (Les Femmes Folles Books, 2017)

Women Write Resistance: Poets Resist Gender Violence (Hyacinth Girl Press, 2013)

Letterpress Collections

Unclose the Door (Gold Quoin Press, 2012)

Farm Hands (Gold Quoin Press, 2012)

Chapbooks

Diversions (Dancing Girl Press, 2019)

Threnody (Porkbelly Press, 2014)

The Bottle Opener (Red Dashboard, 2014)

Spindrift (Dancing Girl Press, 2014)

Stranger Still (Finishing Line Press, 2013)

First Wife (Hyacinth Girl Press, 2013)

Men and Their Whims (Writing Knights Press, 2013)

She Who Loves Her Father (Dancing Girl Press, 2012)

Branding Girls (Finishing Line Press, 2011)

Ghost Girl (Pudding House, 2010)

My Imaginary (Dancing Girl Press, 2010)

www.ingramcontent.com/pod-product-compliance
Lightning Source LLC
Chambersburg PA
CBHW031503040426
42444CB00007B/1195
* 9 7 8 1 6 0 9 6 2 2 4 2 8 *